PA

JOURNEYS OF ADVENTURE

TOLD BY CARINE MACKENZIE
ILLUSTRATIONS BY FRED APPS

Copyright © 1999 Carine Mackenzie
ISBN: 978-1-85792-465-7
Reprinted 2004, 2007 and 2009
Published by Christian Focus Publications, Geanies House,
Tain, Fearn, Ross-shire, IV20 1TW, Scotland, U.K.
www.christianfocus.com
Printed in China

Paul's life was completely changed when God spoke to him on his journey to Damascus. (You can read the whole story in another Biblewise book called Saul – 'The Miracle on the Road.')

Even his name was changed from Saul to Paul.

God sent Paul to travel to many interesting places to preach the Good News of the Gospel.

He travelled through the whole of the island of Cyprus with his friend Barnabas and their helper Mark. There Paul preached the Gospel and in spite of opposition the governor believed in Jesus.

At Lystra Paul and Barnabas met a crippled man who had never been able to walk. He listened intently as Paul spoke. When Paul looked at him he knew that this man had faith to be healed so he called out, 'Stand up on your feet!'

Immediately the man jumped up and started to walk.

The crowds of people were so impressed that they foolishly thought that Paul and Barnabas were gods and they wanted to worship them. This upset Paul and Barnabas very much. 'We are only men like you,' they protested. 'Do not worship us. Worship the living God who made the heavens and the earth and who gives you everything you need.'

Before long the mood of the crowd had completely changed and instead they were hurling stones at Paul. He was dragged out of the city and left for dead but with the help of some friends he got up and went back to Lystra.

Paul was joined by Silas for his next big trip. Young Timothy came along with them too. They went from town to town encouraging churches and teaching the people.

They were guided by God's Holy Spirit. He prevented them from going north into Bithynia and instead they went down to the seaport of Troas.

During the night Paul had a vision. He saw a man from Macedonia standing and pleading with him, 'Come over to Macedonia and help us.'

Immediately Paul and his travelling companions got ready to sail over the sea to Macedonia in Europe. They believed God wanted them to preach the Gospel there.

When they reached Philippi they stopped there for several days. On the Sabbath they went out of the city to the river side where many women had gathered to pray. Paul preached the word to the group.

Lydia was a business woman whose work was to sell beautiful purple cloth. She knew the teachings of the word of God. On that day God opened the heart of Lydia to accept Paul's message and to become a true believer.

She and her family were baptised. She persuaded Paul and his friends to come to stay at her house.

One day on the way to the prayer meeting, Paul met a slave girl who was possessed by an evil spirit which made her tell fortunes. Her owners made a lot of money from this. She kept following Paul and shouting out 'These men are servants of God who are telling you the way to be saved.' At last Paul turned on her and commanded the evil spirit to come out of her.

At that moment the spirit left her. She could no longer tell fortunes. Her owners were very angry. They grabbed Paul and Silas and dragged them to the market place. They brought them before the judges and accused them of causing a disturbance in the town.

They were stripped and beaten and thrown into prison. The jailer was told to guard them carefully so they were put into the inner cell and their feet were fastened in the stocks.

About midnight Paul and Silas were praying and singing praises to God from their prison cell. The other prisoners were listening to them.

Suddenly a violent earthquake shook the foundations of the prison, the doors flew open and all the chains came loose.

The jailer woke up and when he saw the doors open he was so afraid that his prisoners had escaped that he took out his sword and was about to kill himself. Just in time Paul shouted at him 'Do not hurt yourself. We are all here.'

The jailer called for lights and hurried in to Paul and Silas. He brought them out of their cell and asked a very important question.

'Sirs, what must I do to be saved?'

'Believe on the Lord Jesus Christ and you will be saved,' was Paul's reply.

Then Paul and Silas explained to the jailer and all his family the good news of the Gospel of Jesus Christ. They all believed and were baptised. How happy they were.

The jailer washed Paul and Silas' wounds and had a meal prepared for them.

The next day the judges sent officers to release Paul and Silas. 'You can go now,' they said.

'Not at all,' said Paul. 'We are Roman citizens and we have been beaten and thrown into jail without a trial. Let the judges come themselves and escort us out of the prison.'

The judges were so embarrassed when they heard that Paul and Silas were Roman citizens. They rushed to take them from the jail and politely asked them to leave the city.

Before they left Philippi Paul and Silas made a visit to Lydia's house where they met with the believers once again.

Paul made his way to the great city of Athens. He was very upset to see so many people worshipping idols. Every day he would debate with the religious people in the synagogue and in the market place with anyone who happened to be there.

The educated men of Athens loved to discuss new ideas and they were interested to hear what Paul had to say. So Paul stood up in their meeting place and told them about the great God who had made the heavens and the earth and yet has a care for every person. He warned them that God commands everyone to repent of their sins and that God will judge the world justly.

When Paul told them that Jesus Christ had risen from the dead, some of the listeners sneered but others wanted to hear more about it. A few people did truly believe the message of the Gospel that Paul preached.

From Athens Paul moved on to Corinth. There he stayed with Priscilla and Aquila. They were tentmakers like Paul so he worked at this trade with them.

Every Sabbath he would go to the synagogue to reason with the Jews and the Greeks about the Gospel of Jesus Christ. He preached faithfully that Jesus was indeed the Christ but the Jews did not believe him.

From then on Paul no longer went to the synagogue but instead preached in the house next door. Some whole families heard the word there and believed and were baptised. One night God spoke to Paul in a dream telling him not to be afraid. 'Keep on speaking my message,' God said. 'I am with you. No one will harm you. I have many people in this city.'

So Paul stayed for a year and a half teaching the word of God.

Paul preached in many towns and cities. In some places he was well received and the church grew and prospered. In some places the people objected to his message and made trouble for Paul.

Paul and his companions stayed in the port of Troas for a week. The evening before they were due to leave, Paul preached to the company in an upstairs room. A young lad called Eutychus sat on the open window ledge listening to Paul. Paul had so much to say to the people that he talked on and on until midnight. Eutychus was so sleepy, he drifted off into a deep sleep and fell right down to the ground from the upstairs window.

He was picked up dead. Paul came down and threw himself on the young man, putting his arms around him. 'Don't be alarmed,' he said. 'He's alive.'

They went back upstairs again, shared bread together and carried on speaking until dawn. Paul then had to leave and Eutychus went home safe and well.

Paul returned to Jerusalem where he was warmly received by the church. But before long Paul was in trouble once again and put into prison once more.

A band of evil men plotted to kill Paul but his young nephew heard about this scheme and was able to warn Paul and the commander. Paul was moved from Jerusalem to Caesarea at night to keep him from being attacked.

Paul told his story to one official after the other. Felix the governor listened for a bit but was afraid to deal with the matter. 'I'll send for you again when it suits me,' he said but never did.

Festus his successor discussed the matter with King Agrippa. Paul reasoned with them too but eventually the decision was taken – Paul must go to Rome where Caesar himself would deal with the matter.

So Paul set sail for Rome in the charge of a Roman centurion called Julius. The ship put into shore at Sidon and Paul was allowed to go and visit his friends. The route took them north of Cyprus and at Myra in Asia they changed ships. Progress was slow and difficult as the wind was blowing them off course. The journey was becoming more and more dangerous.

At the harbour of Fair Havens on the island of Crete, Paul warned Julius, 'I can see this voyage ending in disaster. We should stay here.'

But Julius didn't listen to Paul's advice and the decision was taken to sail on. In the middle of the Adriatic Sea they hit a big storm.

The ship could make no headway and was tossed along with the hurricane force winds. The ship's lifeboat had to be hoisted from the water to stop it being shattered. The winds were battering the boat so much that the sailors started to throw the cargo overboard to lighten the load. On the third day they even threw over some of the ship's equipment. The storm was so fierce that they all gave up hope of ever being saved.

Paul reminded them of his advice from the safe port in Crete. 'But don't despair,' he urged. 'None of

us will be lost. Only the ship will be destroyed. An angel of the Lord spoke to me last night and told me that all the lives on the ship will be spared. I have faith in God that it will happen as he told me.'

After fourteen nights out in the open sea the sailors sensed that they were nearing land. They took soundings and sure enough the sea was becoming shallower. Now the danger of being wrecked on the rocks was looming closer.

The sailors dropped four anchors from the stern of the boat and prayed for daylight. They thought they would make a break for it and tried to put the lifeboat back into the sea while pretending to work at the anchors.

Paul boldly confronted the centurion, 'Unless these men stay with the ship, we will not be saved.'

So the soldiers cut the ropes to the lifeboat and tossed it into the waves. Before dawn Paul urged everyone to have something to eat. He took some bread, gave thanks to God for it and the others took courage from him and did the same.

When daylight came they could see a bay with a sandy beach. Before the ship could reach the shore it stuck fast in a sand-bar. The ship was broken in pieces by the pounding waves.

Those who could swim jumped overboard and made for land. The others kept afloat on planks and broken pieces of the ship.

All reached land safely.

When they reached land they discovered that the island was Malta. The islanders treated them very kindly. They built a fire on the shore to warm them in the cold and rain.

Paul gathered up a pile of brushwood and as he put it on the fire a snake appeared and attached itself to his hand. The islanders thought this was a sign that Paul must be an evil man.

When Paul shook the snake off into the fire and was none the worse they changed their minds and thought he was a god.

Paul and his party were well looked after by the chief official of Malta. Many sick people including the chief official's father were healed of various diseases after Paul had prayed to God for them.

After three months another ship was ready to sail to Italy. At last Paul reached the city of Rome. Paul was there as a prisoner but he was allowed to live by himself in a house with a soldier to guard him.

Paul preached boldly in Rome and some who heard the Gospel believed on the Lord Jesus Christ. For two years Paul was able to preach and teach about Jesus in his prison house.

The same Gospel that Paul preached is still being preached today and is still changing lives. Some places in our world still need to hear the good news about Jesus. Missionaries like Paul are needed today to go to tell how God so loved the world that he gave his only Son to die for sinners on the cross. Those who believe that will have everlasting life.